A Village of
Poetry People

ISBN: 979-8-89031-297-6 (sc)
ISBN: 979-8-89031-298-3 (hc)
ISBN: 979-8-89031-299-0 (e)

One Galleria Blvd., Suite 1900, Metairie, LA 70001
1-888-421-2397

Dedication

To Kath. Though in spite of a very busy life, made time to get me started on this book.

To Julia, who stepped in when Kath became ill with back pain. and who is as unsparing with her time and patience.

To June, my sister who inspired me with the whole venture, Thank you girls!!

Table of Contents

Preface

The Book

The human race is one large book,
And people are its pages,
I write with fascination about
their stories through the ages.

This is my poetry, and my passion,
and one that's never out of fashion.

The Owl

An owl sat on a withered tree
and did no more than look at me,
So I returned his yellow stare
very pleased to see him there.
He said 'Too wit,' and then 'Too woo',
which could be owl for 'Who are you?
Then silently he flew away
to look for unsuspecting prey.

Ethel's Caller

She was reading her horoscope, and sipping her tea
When she heard a loud knock on the door,
Which she opens to find The Grim Reaper stands there,
She very near fell to the floor.

He apologised for not giving notice
As it wasn't his intended address;
But someone had resuscitated one of his clients,
Leaving his files in a mess.

"Being as your life's not exciting,
And I have a vacuum to fill,
Maybe we could help each other out?
I can arrange for you to be ill.

You can choose from a variety of ailments,
Perhaps something to take you off quick,
I'll make sure that it isn't too painful
You won't have to waste time being sick.

I'll make sure that you won't have to worry,
There really is nothing to dread
I could do you a painless transition
It's not all that bad being dead.

You don't mind if I call you Ethel?
It would look lovely on a headstone,
There are coffins half price in the high street
With handles of brass or of chrome.

I've made you a good proposition,
Please say I'm not wasting my breath,
For if I go back with the numbers intact
I'm promoted to Angel Of Death."

Ethel was feeling her blood pressure rise
As she stared at the insolent ghoul,
Who did it think it was talking about,
Did she look like three kinds of a fool?

"I think you'll be needing the coffin,
You don't look in the greatest of health,
You're as grey as a sheet and as thin as a rake
You should take better care of yourself.

Just listen to me Mr Reaper,
You don't mind if I call you, 'Grim',
My horoscope says I'll be changing my ways
I'm expecting a lottery win.

You can take yourself out of my door way,
Before I start blowing a fuse,
I'll not have you planning my future for me
I'm off on a holiday cruise."

"I'm sorry you feel that way Ethel,
The ghoul said with a terrible grin;
But I'm not going back empty handed
What condition's the man next door in?"

Doing Our Bit

I asked my friend Joan, not to talk on the phone
there's a danger we'll be overheard,
I'm told the Prime Minister's government spies
are listening to our every word.

It seems there's a gadget high in the sky
for spying on you and on me,
It's very efficient, for some people say
it can tell what you've had for your tea.

Our Arthur's corns must be very important
for the PM to pay such attention,
plus my arthritic knees and galloping dandruff
and other things too much to mention.

He claims he is looking for terrorist folk,
and thinks one might drop in for lunch,
We can't be too careful, I've heard people say
that they are an unsavoury bunch

The Prime Minister knows what's got to be done,
We pay him enough to find out,
So listening to our conversation must be
the way to keep terrorists out.

Lamp Light

The lamp in the window is shining and bright,
It lights up the darkness, it glows through the night,
embracing a stranger alone in the dark
enveloping him in it's comforting spark,
It serves to remind him he's far from his home,
But the warmth of the light tells him he's not alone

The Oak

One savage blow from the angry gale
a giant oak fell to the ground, shaking the earth,
while it's splintered branches
gave off a painfilled dying sound.

Standing where the tree once stood
I looked up at the tortured sky,
The canopy of green had gone,
How easily a tree could die.

Four hundred years the tree had been
a home for birds, shelter for men,
T'would take four hundred years, or more
to reach that height and breadth again.

Heroes and Villains

I love to see old movies where the hero's big and hairy
And the heroine is small and blonde, looking like a fairy,
The villain strides across the screen with moustache six foot wide,
Doing many dirty deeds, until he's satisfied.

And then our hero storms about and swings the villain round
He grabs him by his six foot 'tache, and throws him to the ground.
The heroine then screams and wails, she faints, just like a toff,
A lady friend, to bring her round, cuts her corsets off.

I'm choking on my popcorn, (I really hate the stuff)
but it's helping me to concentrate, the men are getting rough.
Our swooning lady's carted out, the villain's laid out cold,
The hero wins the lady, because he's big and bold.

Now I'm going home to Fred, screaming kids and cat,
I'll never be a heroine ... so I suppose that's that.

Soul Mate

Have you seen my other half?
(I haven't met him yet)
I often have the notion that he's playing hard to get,
Some days he's ahead of me, some days he's behind,
I've hunted for a long time, he's very hard to find.
He looks for me , I look for him, we're looking past each other,
We look so hard we cannot see the prospect of a lover.
So here we have half a man hopping down the street,
He won't have a leg to stand on when I sweep him off his feet.

A Last Ambition

If I should die before I wake
I hope I've had my share of 'cake',
I hope I laughed myself to death
through a happy lack of breath.

No doubt I found my pot of gold,
You'll hear I died both rich and old,
I hope the coroner reports
'Good heavens! what a cheerful corpse'.

And if you're driving in your car,
look at the sky and see a star,
and should you smile at what you see
then want to laugh spontaneously,

Well..that's because the star is me.

The Stranger

I look into your face
and see a stranger there,
For you return my gaze
with a blank then puzzled stare.

We have known each other
for the longest time,
The fact that we are strangers
has no reason, has no rhyme.

Have we not been together
through the good times, and the bad?
Shared a wealth of feeling,
being happy, being sad.

I'm looking at you once again
but see no loving glance,
We could both be something more
given half a chance.

Can strangers build a friendship
If we make each moment pay?
Turning from the mirror
I sadly walk away.

A Feeling

I had a lovely feeling, complete and without words,
It soared as though to touch the sky, freer than the birds.

It swooped over the treetops, fluttered through each leaf,
Then circled every blade of grass beneath.

And so to leap! cavorting through the crystal air
Moving!, shifting! dancing! without care.

It had a need to touch all life, to swell with joy, and song,
And then to own, to touch and to belong.

It flows across the emerald land, reaching the outer shore,
To breathe the scent of land and sea, and more.

Enveloping the ocean, kissed the waves that rocked the sea,
Enriched, it brings its essence back to me.

A Boozy Tale

Bill staggers home from the Bricklayers Arms,
(He'd just been thrown out of the door)
'Not very friendly', he says to himself
as he picks himself up off the floor.

He weaves his way home, but loses direction
so sat himself under a tree,
Squinting through bleary eyes he says to himself
'There's a small creature looking at me'.

'I'm a beer fairy' said the strange little sprite,
'It's my job to take care of the hops,
But I hear you've been giving good beer a bad name
do I waste my time tending the crops'?

'I'm employed by the Overall Guardian of booze
to see that they make a good beer.
But I think I've been busy wasting my time
when I look at the sight of you here.'

'It's rewarding to see humans laugh and relax
while supping a sparkling ale.
But watching you drowning yourself in the stuff
my love for the job's growing stale.'

I think the times come to change my career
and do something else with my time,
So I'm ending my contract, and telling the Guardian
I'm transferring over to wine.

Words

The voice set sail on a sea of words,
The tide of words was rough.
The mind, the captain of the words
felt the going tough,
It touched the rocks of conflict
but found no harbour there,
'Til the winds of reason turned the tide
and made the going fair.

The Burglar

A figure prowls the darkening street,
looking to ply his trade,
Seeking out an easy kill,
a living has to be made.
Searching with a practised eye
he sees a house that stands alone,
Instinctively, he can tell
there is no-one at home.

With breathless stealth he slithers through
a broken window at the rear,
'Such carelessness', he tells himself,
'will cost the owner very dear.'
Once inside he pauses,
whilst adjusting to the gloom
His vision clears, he finds himself
inside a shabby room,
Checking every exit,
before he starts the task,
He slips a glove on either hand,
and then secures his mask.

Seasoned fingers flicker through
the items all around,
Soon it was clear there wasn't much
of value to be found,
'There must be something worth my time,'
he mutters to himself,
Then spies a shiny object
standing on a nearby shelf.

It is in fact a photograph
inside a silver frame,
Discard the trash, is the rule
of his thieving game,
He tears the photo' from its frame
and tossed it to the floor,
Then a second glance took hold of him
and shook him to his core,
'This face could be my Grandfather',
he stares in disbelief,
As hot tears burn the eyes of this
unrepentant thief.

Amazed at his reaction,
he tries to leave the room
But a searing pain disables him
to fill his soul with doom,
Buried grief tore through him
to hurl him back through time,
Instantly he saw himself
the tender age of nine.

Now images unbidden
are flashing through his mind,
In a loveless life he has found
one person who is kind,
No-one before had smiled at him,
or ever called him son,
He feels a warmth he's never known,
A new life has begun

And he remembers how
he would always long to please
This kindly generous old man
with failing eyes, and knees,
GRANDAD! 'look what I have made'
'Bring it here my boy'
He swelled with pride as grandad praised
his clumsily made toy.

The image changes,
showing he is running home from school,
'Come straight home, don't dawdle'
was the one and only rule,
'I'M HOME GRANDAD' he hollers,
but there is no answering call,
Instead he finds the old man lying
crumpled in the hall,
'Wake Up Grandad!! he shakes him hard,
Wake Up! It's Me! I'm Home!!
But the only sound he's hearing,
is a strangely muffled moan.

The image changes once again,
a policeman holds his hand,
He's wondering what he's done wrong,
and doesn't understand,
He's taken to a large dark house,
and told to wait inside,
The aching loneliness returns,
he hides his face and cries.

The waiting turns from days to years,
the dark place now his home,
So as the happy memories died,
his young heart turned to stone,
Now he sees with adult eyes what
no-one else would say,
His Grandad couldn't take him home,
because he'd died that day.

Realisation of this truth
cut through him like a knife
The man, who clearly loved him,
who'd taught him to love life
Hadn't left him to his fate,
but stayed until the end,
This man, who was his father,
his grandfather, and his friend.

He's seeing what he could have been,
and what he has become,
The thief sat on a strangers floor
is not Grandfathers son,
Burning shame replaces grief,
his life has been a lie,
Relentless memories have shown
his young self slowly die,

The bubble bursts, his brain has cleared,
He's horrified to see,
the room, the bag of stolen goods,
'Is this really me?!!
Panicking, he takes the bag
and throws it's contents wide,
Leaping towards the window,
he is once again outside,

As the cool night air refreshes him,
he hears that loving voice;
'When it comes to life my boy,
you always have a choice'
Don't lose sight of who you are,
keep that memory bright',
Heaving a sigh of thankfulness,
He slips into the night.

The Bogeyman

The Bogeyman will get you, he's waiting in the hall,
Or he's standing on the landing, every night he comes to call,
So if you're not asleep at night, very still, with eyes shut tight
you will be a sorry sight, the Bogeyman will get you.

Auntie Vi' would tell this tale, as I went off to bed,
She's not keen on psychology, and so I used to dread
the thought of sleeping at her house in case I woke up dead
And find she's right! the Bogeyman has got me.

At the tender age of ninety three, you'd think I've found a cure,
For the Bogeyman is not around to scare me anymore,
I climb the stairs still full of fright, so will you please leave
on the light, or else the dreaded ghostly sprite
Of Auntie Vi' will get me.

The Exile

They seek him here, they seek him there,
The taxman's searching everywhere
But Uncle Nigel's gone to ground
he's making sure he can't be found.

He thinks their peevish attitude
is envy, or is very rude,
He feels the taxmans far too keen
for always bursting on the scene.

And often asks 'what have you got?'
Begrudging me my second yacht,'
'Why can't the fellow go away'?
We hear poor Uncle Nigel say.

He's gone to live a long way off,
His island home's fit for a toff,
The taxman will not find him there
He's keeping quiet..'it's only fair'.

The Major

Major Eyeswater met young Liza Lott
in a bar on a Saturday night,
With her long curly hair and baby blue eyes
the Major was smitten on sight.

He wined her and dined her and bought her
the best of luxuries he could afford,
When he looked at his lovely he felt he could say
he'd at last found the one he adored.

So he was a little taken aback when Liza
ran off with his friend,
She had taken his house, his money, his all,
for Liza just knew how to spend.

Now he's left alone with his memories of Liza
her devious deeds they were many.
And all he has left is his friend and his cat,
What Friend!! he doesn't have any.

Miss Jones

The year's 1940, the person Miss Jones, a girl of inferior charm,
Her peers have described her as not very bright,
with an aura of tedious calm,
Her childhood was spent at a good boarding school,
where the pupils were taught to relate,
But the girls in her class seemed to bypass Miss Jones
every time, at a furious rate.

Her dream was to captain the schools Hockey team,
but she never stood out in a crowd,
So her inconsequentiality meant
she never had cause to be proud.
When her schooldays were over she thought she might try
to find a position in law,
With a talent for languages spurring her on,
might bring her prestige to the fore,

Her position was blighted in just the same way
as it had been when she was at school,
For instead of her joining a Law Firm Elite,
ended up in a large typing pool.
At a huge office party she wandered around
listening in on important folk,
Should they acknowledge her presence at all
would dismiss her remarks as a joke.

A Member of Parliament crossing the floor
chanced to trip over Miss Jones,
'Sorry my dear for not seeing you there,
I hope there are no broken bones',
He apologetically offered a glass of champagne,
asking 'what is your role in the war'
So pleased to be seen, she said she was keen
to do any ministry chore.

Soon they were talking of Hitler and such,
what a mess he was making of things,
So if she was looking for wartime pursuits
he could possibly pull a few strings,
The Secret Service is short of a spy,
as one has gone down with flu'
I could put your name forward this minute my dear,
if you think it's the right job for you.

She's immediately packed off to 'Somewhere in France'
to help sort this German thing out,
And has made up her mind on behalf of the King,
to eliminate this bossy Kraut.
She's supposed to liaise with an Underground Group,
who have kept Hitler tied up in knots,
But as no-one came forward to acknowledge her,
she assumed that maybe they'd forgot.

Looking about her she spies a large group
of folk filing in through a door,
Joining the queue she's pushed into a room
Where the Fuhrer's discussing the war,
Walking around she suddenly found
herself mingling with Hitler's elite,
They move to a table laden with food,
she follows and takes up a seat,

Our Miss inconsequential displays
her potential when sat next to Hitler at lunch,
With some coarse Nazi chaps, (drinking something called Schnapps)
which she thought an unsavoury bunch,
Due to her boring Aura, they have to ignore her,
and talk of their conquering skills,
First they'll flatten Europe, then flatten Old England
for the exersize and for the thrills.

She silently listens unheard and unseen
to the devious doings they've planned,
She'd learnt excellent German from a boyfriend called Herman
which enabled her to understand,
She knew she must contact the Underground group
but didn't know how to proceed
Then saw their address in the Resistance Gazette,
so set out with the greatest of speed.

The Underground Group were enjoying their cocoa
when Miss Jones knocked on the door,
She burst in amongst them, and told them the story,
for now they must all know the score,
Some were wide eyed, but some were distrustful,
'How could she access Hitlers den',
If you're the wrong sort of spy, it's easy to die,
so she showed her credentials to them,

A message from London confirmed her credentials,
(she's pleased she won't have to be shot),
Her new friends discuss the best way to employ her,
so fashion a devious plot.
At last she's found friends who admire, even envy,
her talent for not being seen,
Now she can fulfill her longing to shine,
be the best spy that there's ever been.

Miss Jones ghostly exploits amongst the Gestapo,
explode on intelligence ears,
Reports back from France, cause the Warlords to dance,
She's evaporated all their worst fears.
Each detailed report that came to their office
left the Top Brass in awe,
If Miss Jones speaks of happenings somewhere or sometime,
she was someone you mustn't ignore

The Gestapo is flummoxed, 'There must be a Traitor
accessing our top secret plans',
They even developed suspicions of Hitler,
some papers were by his own hands,
The Brits were delighted!, the Germans were livid!
so set out to find this bold spy,
Storm troopers were ordered to flush out the problem,
or Hitler will want to know why,

The fearsome storm troopers invaded their hideout,
bringing a feeling of doom,
They drag out her comrades, yawns in Miss Jones direction,
then leave her behind in the gloom,
She contacted London to tell of events,
saying 'no-one is left here but me'
Her tedious aura has come to her rescue
leaving her active and free.

The Allies agreed, this valuable agent
has altered the course of the war
As her flawless reporting and accurate detail
has made Hitler's nose bloody sore,
At last the war's over, leaving Miss Jones
with a thrilling story to tell,
Both King and the Country are proud of the hero
they're calling the 'New Pimpernel'.

She lands in an airfield 'Somewhere in England',
and taken to meet the Top Brass
Who whisk her away to Buckingham Palace,
(she feels somewhat out of her class,)
A ceremony has been arranged in her honour,
to acknowledge her courage and skill,
That the King wants to decorate her for her effort
is to Miss Jones the ultimate thrill.

Miss Jones steps forward to claim her reward
as a tea lady comes through the door,
Becoming entangled, they trip over her trolley
and fall in a heap on the floor,
Hurrying over, the King shows concern
on hearing their embarrassed cries,
He rescues the Tea lady, pins on the Medal
Saying; "Miss Jones! What a clever disguise!!"

Charlie.

Charlie is a Lurcher,
He is handsome, sleek, and black.
He has the longest tail and legs,
he has the longest back.

There's one thing he's not fond of,
it's riding in a car,
But if we let him have his way
we wouldn't go too far.

Then we hit on a solution,
(It pleases me to please,)
For he really likes to chase ahead
and stretch his doggy knees

So we tied him to the bumper,
roared up to sixty on the clock,
but to see our Charlie overtake,
gave us quite a shock.

Possession

Please stay in my life sweet love
it hurts that you should leave,
You are the joy that lifts my soul
my breaking heart will grieve
And I will cry a thousand tears
my life be filled with empty years
    If you should go.

I have lingered far too long
Betrayed my hearts desire,
The need to leave is growing strong
and burns with passions fire,
I have to live a life that's true,
even though I'm missing you,
    I have to go.

That I remain it would be wrong
It pains me should I stay
My life would be an empty song
My being cold and grey
Although I love you like no other
I'm thirty six.. I'm leaving mother.
    I must go.

Sid's So-lil-oquy

I do wish our Lil' wouldn't let herself go
said Sid as he waddled downstairs,
He glanced in the mirror, adjusted his teeth
then tightened the belt on his flares.

To look at her now, it's hard to see how
she's the woman I used to adore.
Bending over the mat he mooned at the cat
as he picked up the mail by the door.

"A slovenly wife is a harrowing sight
it causes a fellow to grieve,"
He said, guzzling down a can full of ale
then wiping his mouth on his sleeve.

"When a man's in his prime, a wife should take time
to make sure that her husband won't stray,
She should turn on the smiles, and the womanly wiles
to keep all her rivals at bay.

But she wrinkles her nose when she picks up my clothes,
her back aches when she brings me my tea,
I wonder what makes her so dissatisfied
it's her duty to take care of me.

Why can't she be more like Deidre next door
who's always attractive to men,
They're coming and going, their numbers are growing
I've counted at least about ten,

Hmm, that's a nice car just pulled up outside
probably here to take Deirdre a ride,
Here she comes now all dressed up to kill,
if it wasn't for the fur coat I'd think it was Lil'

Why Lil'! It is you! What's the meaning of this?
and now she is giving the driver a kiss,
She told me that kissing gave her a bad head
and here she is kissing that bookmaker Ted.

Hang on there Lil' you're married to me,
you can't leave like this, I've not had my tea.
They're driving away, it just isn't right
She's waving two fingers 'til they're out of sight,

Such an ungrateful woman, it's just my bad luck,
Wait a minute! ... I wonder if Deidre can cook.

An Excellent Man

I met a man the other day, he said 'I'm ninety five
I flew Spitfires in the last world war, and I'm glad to be alive',
I listened to his story, as he spoke his eyes shone bright
his voice alive with passion at the memory of the fight.

Then finding fame in broadcasting, he led a busy life,
But took the time to marry his one and only wife,
Now he's here, a frail old man standing in the park,
but just one glance told me he hasn't lost his spark,

I found we both loved poetry, the bold and fiery kind,
he said it gave him comfort, and helped to free his mind,
I said I loved 'The Highwayman', reciting the first verse
He joined in with the second as though we had rehearsed.

And so we stood together the Spitfire man and me,
throwing verses at each other, and laughing loud with glee.

Politicking

The public asked the minister,
'Please try not to be sinister,
but can we have some work
so we might buy a loaf of bread?'

The minister told his Secret'ry
'To try and see what he could see
Who told the public'what's the fuss
you're not exactly dead',

Said the public to the secret'ry
'your answers not the best for me,
now I must use my vote with
the brains inside my head.'

'So tell your boss we're very cross,
and that you both will feel the loss
when we take time to see you
both politically dead'.

Dracula's Dilemma

Dracula sits in the Gravediggers Arms,
drinking a large Bloody Mary,
He's confiding to Igor his servant and friend,
That life has become very scary.

"Humans are not looking after their blood,
in the old days I felt more secure,
I could bite on a virgin without any urging,
Her blood would be tasty and pure.

Today I am thinking I've found a pure maid,
But the lady's not quite what she seems,
Mother didn't say I would suffer this problem
It's giving me nightmarish dreams.

I recently bit on a modern day 'virgin'
She seemed to look tasty and meek,
But was so full of pot, my system was shot,
I was stuck in my coffin all week.

I thought a blood bank might be a solution
To drink all day long without trying,
But the thought of it not coming from a young neck
Didn't seem to be so satisfying

I found an old virgin ('which ought to be safer,)
curled up and asleep in her bed,
But the mountain of pills she took for her ills
Made me wonder why she wasn't dead.

Even old ladies are drugged to the eyeballs,
And so to preserve my good health,
There really is only one true safety measure,
I'll just have to bite on myself.

The Ghoul's Holiday

The ghouls were taking a week off from haunting,
They found that they needed a break once a year,
It was sometimes exhausting scaring the mortals
especially the spoilsports who weren't into fear,

They had rented a castle down at the seaside
to do some moon bathing and get a moontan,
It was something they'd copied watching the human,
It did fascinate them, the antics of man.

They chat about ghouling and its consequences,
A millennium's haunting had ceased to be fun
One ghoul complained people don't frighten easy,
If I wasn't so dead I'd say pass me the gun.

A pub haunting ghoul said he'd thought of retiring
the landlord ignores me, I'm bad for the trade,
The locals were happy drowning their sorrows
even the ones who drank neat lemonade.

Another ghoul spoke up, telling his story
his talent was howling and clanking the chains,
But as TV gave humans free horror channels
he was feeling outclassed by 'The Fiend In The Drain',

A lady ghoul wondered where her life was going
Her screaming was famous for chilling the blood.
but her fame is in tatters, for nobody listens
now the lady's depressed and feels misunderstood.

They all agreed Dracula has the same problem.
and they had to admit he's the master of fright,
What is to be done if the Master can't hack it,
We'd best all go home, and let's a call it a night.

Quiet Time

As I wandered out in the cool morning air,
The world seemed at peace, not a whisper of care,
A blackbirds song swells from a tree as I pass,
treading my way over sweet scented grass.

Then shattering sounds set my eardrums on fire,
who is the culprit? some mad fiend for hire?
Why it's Henry McHenry ... that guru of noise
Revving his bike with a gang of loud boys,

The blackbird has flown, leaving feathers behind,
But Henry and cohorts appear not to mind,
He's sat on his Norton, a present from dad.
Who buys only the best for his noisemonger lad.

The McHenrys should have their windows insured,
To guard against Henry, who hates to be bored.
Tonight he'll be out, seeing some of the sights,
Ignoring the traffic, and jumping the lights.

He roars down the motorway doing a ton,
The faster he races, the better the fun,
He tears along feeling so happy and free,
Until he's waylaid by a giant oak tree,

Our poor boy is in traction, (not looking so hard,)
His bike ended up at the local scrapyard,
So here's a sad tale of one more disaster
Where the hero is covered, (not in glory) but plaster.

As I wandered out in the cool morning air,
The world seemed at peace, not whisper of care,
A blackbirds song swells from a tree as I pass,
treading my way over sweet scented grass.

A Stray Kitten's Prayer

I'll love you for life if you'll love me
Will you take me and give me a home?
I would cherish the comfort of shelter and friendship
I might not survive on my own.

One small corner is all I am needing
I wouldn't take very much space,
and just a small bed to rest my tired head.
a warm haven to call my own place,

For a morsel of food, I'll repay you
You will not regret being kind
I'll make sure that your house hasn't one single mouse
for giving me such piece of mind.

Another World

There's a cupboard that needs to be tidied,
Though my visits are terribly rare,
I've avoided this place for too long a time
The cupboard that's under the stair.

So biting the bullet I open the door
and cautiously peer in the gloom,
I timidly tread it's mysterious depths
it seems like the families junk tomb,

I reach for the light switch, and gaze at the scene
that's a cluttered cobwebby surprise
'Things' half remembered, 'things' long forgot.
languish in front of my eyes.

Here's grandmas old slipper she never could find,
and the top set of grandads false teeth,
The loss left him lisping each time that he swore,
so stopped swearing, which caused him much grief.

Wow! here's Mr Wainwright, and his typist Rose,
who've been missing a year and a day
They seem to be happy hid under my nose.
I've a feeling they're both here to stay.

There are signs that Lord Lucan had taken refuge,
here's a monogrammed sock just for proof.
It's making me wonder whoever, whatever's
been hiding away 'neath my roof.

I've decided to leave but can't find the door,
I shout loud,' Is there anyone there?'
Have I become part of a weird twilight zone
in the cupboard that's under the stair.

Boot Blues

I once was in the best of health,
Gleaming on a posh shop shelf,
My supple leather's pretty blue,
When disaster strikes, I'm owned by you.

You obviously bought me for a treat
to clothe your knobbly Sasquatch feet,
My poor stretched leather's gone to grief,
the lacings look like gritted teeth,

From pristine shop to muddy fields
I squelch, and my poor leather yields,
The pretty blue has turned sludge brown,
Why don't you like to walk in town?

Now looking like two clods of earth
no-one can see how much I'm worth,
Mangled by two steaming feet;
no longer pretty blue and neat.

The Rider

He loves to ride his motorbike, roaring here and there,
Just sitting in the saddle, he's a man without a care,
He's free from all confinement. This champion of steel
not imprisoned in a motor car, a limp hand on the steering wheel.

He wears a bright green safety mack' so all can see him pass,
Not so much for safety, it highlights his style and class,
He weaves in and out of traffic, demonstrating he's a star.
amid bleeping horns and curses emanating from each car.

Tearing down a country lane, he knows he's hard to catch,
rounding a bend discovers he has hit a greasy patch.
catapulted through the air both bike and him do part
Landing in a nearby field, he breaks his neck, and stops his heart.

A passing motorist finds him there and calls the police for aid,
The policeman shook his head to see the sorry sight displayed,
then turns to steer the crowds away, and growing pile of traffic,
'He was easily found' the motorist said 'in his bright green safety jacket'

Adoration

Your eyes are like the softest rays of light at early dawn,
Your hair, a miracle of gold like summer ripened corn,
The world has nothing to reflect your loveliness and youth,
Glancing in the mirror I could see he spoke the truth.

Different Loves

Countess Esmeralda 'Brown'.
was the most pampered cat in town.
To Mr. Brown she was a Queen.
the finest cat there'd ever been,
He fed to her the best of fish,
and served it on a silver dish,
then as he stroked her fur (like silk)
poured her the cream from off the milk.

The world could see Countess was fat..
not a good thing for a cat,
She never stepped outside the house,
to catch a rat, a vole, or mouse,
instead she lazed the hours away,
'til Mr Brown brought her a tray
filled up with such exotic food,
that satisfied her every mood.

Her life might just have stayed the same,
until a tomcat, with no name
whose scarred face looked as though he might
have been in every sort of fight.
leapt (through the window) at her feet,
he thought as cats go she looked sweet
and showed her that he'd do no harm,
he seemed to have a worldly charm.

She's coaxed by him to come outside,
to see a world that's big and wide,
They played upon the tiles all night,
the exersize was pure delight
He rather liked this feline lass,
and pleased he'd found a touch of class.
and she thought that his gypsy ways
might liven up her empty days.

But he's moved on and she's gone too,
poor Mr. Brown is feeling blue.
Her velvet cushion empty now,
he's wondering why she left and how.

Jim's Problem

To hear Jim's conversation you'd think he's only has one limb,
He thinks his nether regions are the major part of him,
They try to change the subject, friends of his who care
But after just two minutes interval he wears a vacant stare.

Diverse conversation has its own reward,
but nothing seems to stop his thoughts heading netherward,
We decide to talk religion, a safe subject we hope
To find we are discussing nether regions of the pope.

His feeble concentration means he mustn't drive a train,
Or, on the grounds of health and safety he must never fly a plane,
He made an application for a job he longed to do,
A firm refusal told him bomb disposal's not for you.

I wouldn't like the thought of Jim coming to my aid
So I'm glad he's not a member of the local Fire Brigade,
We've noticed his affliction is getting out of hand,
And so we'll have to leave him, wandering in Netherland.

Halfway up the Stair

I've found a strange amnesia zone halfway up the stair,
for when I'm standing at the top, I wonder why I'm there,
Little wisps of memory rise, to taunt the brain and tease the eyes
My mind wiped clean.. vacant surprise standing on the stair.

The Singer

Hazel, don't move, Hazel don't breathe,
or the neck of your sweater will cause you to grieve
You're singing a song full of passion and pain
but this garment has not been designed for such strain.

Your cleavage does seem just a tad overdone
though I must admit so far, the sweater has won,
But one more deep breath..and my hypnotised eyes
will bulge from their sockets like your 'obvious prize'.

Please don't sing the high notes .just leave them alone
or some folks might cheer loud, while others might groan.
Though your voice is a sweet one and really quite good.
let's not cheer you for seeing far more than we should.

Bleep

He lay in a puddle of Marston's best bitter
gazing in wonder at a puddle of stars.
As the last pint hit home like the fuel in a rocket
he's convinced that he's landed on cool planet Mars.

A Martian, disguised as a publican landlord
spoke in a language confusing his ears.
Bidding him get to his 'bleep bleeping feet'
or find that the evening would end up in tears.

He's back as an earthling tottering homeward,
It feels like a horse has been kicking his head
His father awaits with a 'bleep bleeping' welcome
and orders him off to his 'bleep bleeping bed'.

Top Cat

A magic ball of tabby fluff slinks out into the night.
to startle any sleeping bird, or give the mice a fright.
She is the queen of our back lawn, and makes it known to all
the prowling tomcats who might think they ought to pay a call,

Like a screeching howling banshee she cuffs them on the ear.
But one Tomcat she favours knows he has no need to fear
her flashing claws and angry jaws. He's far more than a fling,
For she's the queen of our back lawn. it seems he is the king.

Undetected

Sherlock Holmes was worried, in his cool and precise way,
Dr Watson had been missing, for one week and a day,
The Doc' was on an errand buying crumpets for their tea,
So the sleuth's keen mind was troubled wondering
where his friend might be.

A whiff of stale tobacco was usually a clue,
But with no aroma present the clues were rather few.
He found a lot of fingerprints jam coated on the wall.
as that was the Doc's last breakfast, perhaps it was no clue at all.

But maybe our great man was wrong, the prints might tell a tale
of devious doings to his friend, The tracks must not grow stale.
He grabbed his trusty violin, played an inspirational tune.
Which made the dogs for miles around start howling at the moon.

He ceased his music making, for he couldn't stand the din,
and sought a way to rack his brain with beakers full of gin.
What has befallen my dear friend ? I can no longer think,
And little wonder reader, he had drunken all the drink.

The forensic mind was clear once more
as a sunlit daylight dawned,
and blinking through two bleary eyes,
he stretched a bit, and yawned.
he thought he heard an anguished cry.
'Is that you Watson my dear feller?
'Holmes! I've fallen down the coal hole,
and I'm stuck here in the cellar.'

First Kill

I watch the man who is going to die,
I have him in my sights,

And when I'm done, his life is done,
I'll take his days, I'll take his nights.

I'm crouching in a muddy trench
He runs to me as he is bid,

And as he dies I'll tell myself
it's the saddest deed I ever did.

Walkies

I'm standing here waiting and ready. Are you?
What on earth do you mean you can't find your shoe?
I'm always dressed up for whatever I do,
If you don't get a move on the day will be through.

I'm standing here waiting. You crawl 'round the hall.
You've discovered your coat and a badly chewed ball
Do you ever think we will go walking at all?
As the day disappears it will soon be nightfall.

I'm too tired of waiting I'm off to my bed.
We dogs live such short lives I might soon be dead.
This hanging about really makes me sees red,
I'll just slip off to sleep and go walks in my head.

Job Creation

Frankenstein McWerter had invention in his genes,
(For his famous Great Grand daddy would invent beyond his dreams,)
He longed to step from mediocrity into a world of fame,
to be just like Great grandaddy..and make himself a name.

After reading books since childhood of Great Grandads 'morbid deeds',
is the reason why his eager mind began to sow the seeds,
if he could imitate his forebear, to be as bold and bright,
so he worked with curiosity late into each night.

But he began to feel thwarted, for 'materials' were few
and he didn't have the 'contacts' that old granddaddy knew,
Maybe it's time to realise these methods are outdated,
especially as the modern man prefers to be cremated.

And it seems his famous relative was having the last laugh
for when it came to bodysnatching he just couldn't get the staff.
As for 'gleaming laboratories', well that idea was dead.
The closest he could manage was his little garden shed.

His hopes of fame and fortune seemed to wither on the vine,
'It seems the old boy hogged the lot. and none of it is mine'
He couldn't follow in his footsteps, it was such a bitter blow.
So he decided to make waxworks at Tussauds waxwork show.

It was written in his contract that he asked to be released
if the subject of his waxwork wasn't very much deceased.

A Big Ending

'Does my bum look big in this?'
All I did was tell her 'yes!!'
Now suddenly she's raging mad,
How was I to guess.

I suppose I should have held my tongue
and turned the other cheek,
I was tricked by a trick question
She's not spoken for a week.

My parents told me 'tell the truth'
What the hell were they both thinking,
They were stone cold sober at the time,
Dad said it without winking.

It's really playing on my mind
Invading all my dreams
Engulfed by big bums every night
The neighbors hear my screams.

I've had enough of girlfriends
my life's become a mess,
It's time I turned my life around,
I think I'll take up chess.

A Dark God

I came across a fallen God
doing menial chores,
I asked him why. He told me
he had caused too many wars.

He said he got the biggest thrill
from watching humans die,
But sounds that gave him power
was to hear their loved ones cry.

The higher Gods, as punishment
for rejecting human worth,
Banished him, to live amongst
the lowliest on Earth.

So now he sees what humans see,
And feels their pain and cries,
'Til finally, he'll know the pain
of growing old,. then dies.

In a Word

'A Plague On All Their Houses', what a great well rounded curse,
which, if yelled in my direction I'd go looking for a nurse,
The medieval insult was well thought out, with feeling,
designed to cause the knees to knock, and send the senses reeling,

At times they'd use such flowery words, even though intense,
would leave the victim wondering if he should take offense,
Today the insults aren't so grand, a very lukewarm dish,
akin to being slapped around by very limp wet fish.

What if yesterday's youth, and today's youth got together
We can be sure that neither lad would talk about the weather.
'Why doth thou stare so unkempt knave, do I offend thy sight?
'Watch it mush. or I might think you're looking for a fight'

The loss of such rich language causes the brain to shrink,
and if it carries on this way, we'll lose the need to think
So if you want to vent your spleen to try to make me vexed,
do it the medieval way, don't send a timid text.

A Human Condition

Bob Belchers life was blighted
in a most unfortunate way
His body gasses bothered him
at night, and through each day,

He remembered University
whilst collecting his degree
when his accidental thunderclap
resembled World War three,

His life was on a knife edge
playing this discordant tune,
A force of nature which could wilt
a flower in full bloom.

Friends he found, were often
'not at home' if he should call,
his eruptions in their bathroom
made the tiles fall off the wall,

He saw a competition,
It was called the 'Art of Fart'
Thinking he might stand a chance
decided to take part,

He climbed up on the rostrum
his chance to take the crown,
but a nearby smoker took the blast
and burnt the building down.

A local sailor noticed Bob
and immediately was charmed.
This man just might be useful
if my yacht became becalmed.

The pair are such a perfect team,
with Bobs spontaneous 'gales'
They win each cup by pointing
Bob's rear end towards the sails.

Storm Warning

The weather was not in the greatest of moods
with the wind fiercely howling, the loudest I've heard,
Mrs. Brown's hat, and the man next doors cat
were flying away like a jet propelled bird.

The waves they were lashing so high out to sea
as if to try slapping the clouds as they passed,
Like some ancient quarrel with memory forgotten.
But Tess Thompson's annoyed; her new hairdo's been trashed.

Mrs. White is so anxious, her lodgers a sailor,
She hopes he won't drown, and his life isn't spent
She sends up a prayer to bring him back safely,
For the last seven months he has not paid the rent.

I rush to a cafe that stands on the corner,
and order a tea with a toasted teacake,
I'll stay here until the weather's subsided,
It's so cozy; I don't care how long it might take.

Ambition

Will you give me a sign if you want to be mine,
a wink of the eye just might do it,
I like it a lot sitting here on your yacht,
Are you looking for someone to crew it ?

I'd be quiet as a mouse, in your super large house
if you're needing somebody to share,
And I'd feel so alive in that Rolls Royce you drive
once you own up and say that you care.

Oh! you're meeting your wife ..the love of your life,
so this is where our relationship ends,
now we'll call it a day and I'll go on my way,
Er..do you have any rich single friends.

The Haunting

Hello, Aggie dear, did you think I had gone?
I'm here to pay back for the wrongs you have done.
You blighted my earth life you black-hearted hag
The tables are turned, now it's my turn to nag.

In my lifetime you took me for better or worse
for me to discover those words were a curse.
You lied and you cheated your way through our life,
Telling each lover you're nobody's wife.

But now I'm a witness to your cheating game
should lovers desert you they are not to blame.
I'll haunt them until they fly off to another
and you are left crying and run to tell Mother.

This righting of wrongs keeps me tied to the earth
Now it's your turn to feel you're of such little worth.
Your life won't turn out as you'd like it to be
for the only one left by your side will be me..

Mis-Fortune

In actual fact, your Honour, I am an honest man.
So I would like to ask you to be lenient if you can.
In my defense, I went to see a gypsy for a fee
Who,(through her crystal ball) saw good fortune come to me,

She said 'follow your instincts, stay true to how you feel'
so I took the mystics wise advice, and 'felt' I'd like to steal,
It was purely as an exercise, and no more than a prank
while walking down the high street I popped in to rob the bank,

The reason for the gun? Well, I was taking it to mend,
It isn't mine, I sought to do a favour for a friend,
you can see my predicament?, and how I've been misled,
because a careless gypsy put such ideas in my head.

Her irresponsible advice has lead to where I am
Thinking I'd be in the gravy boat, instead I'm in a jam,
Well that's the truth your Honour, it's a shame if I do time
because the gypsy didn't say the fortune wasn't mine.

The Vampires Food Evolution

The Vampires were sitting around the bonfire
enjoying a Halloween supper,
Consisting of sausages, bacon, and chips
then washing it down with a 'cuppa'.

Now that the humans are drunk on fast food
it's essence appears in their blood.
So when vampires are taking a drink from their veins
The 'essence' begins to taste good.

Hamburgers are relished by Vampire elite
who are loving that great meaty tang,
but are having some trouble with trying to eat
as the food's getting speared on each fang.

The Lord of the vampires has suffered the most
and is tending to look rather fat,
he's having a struggle to get off the ground
when he wants to change into a bat.

It seems silver bullets aren't needed these days
Just throw them a meatball instead.
It's a much better method than stakes in the heart,
Quite a kind way to kill the undead.

My Pal

We took a trip.. it wasn't far
out riding in my old grey car,
forgetting we are ??ty two
behaving like we used to do.

We move along a laugh a mile
(just because we make us smile)
The day is bright, and so are we
the open road says we are free.

Around a corner..here we are,
a place to eat..I stop the car,
we've found our 'Never Never Land'
with endless cakes upon a stand.

I choose fruitcake..you choose cream
each cake tasting like a dream.
our fingers sticky..face is too
buried in a gorgeous goo,

The day goes on in happy haze
an echo of our former days
and so we laugh our way back home,
running out of road to roam.

We've been mates a long long time,
that's the reason for this rhyme,
And though you live too far away
that is how it's going to stay.

Maggie

Let me introduce you to Maggie, a girl in a million or more,
She's short on mystic, with a mannish physique,
any boxer would envy her jaw.

She's the athletic sort, who is mad keen on sport,
Her prowess is known far and wide,
She achieved her main dream when she joined the
mens team with a place in the towns rugby side.

She went head to head with the man Fiery Fred
the first time she played in the game,
With her face in the dirt she thought he looks a flirt
and hoped he was thinking the same.

While she mused on this thought his muscles grew taught
as he tossed her over his shoulder,
She fell with a thud, in a puddle of mud,
the exercise made Maggie bolder.

With a leap and a bound she brought him to the ground
he fell with a thundering crash,
Breaking
three ribs,
one nose,
and his skull,
Now the scenes an emergency dash.

She watched as her hero was carried away,
(She thought she'd at last found a lover)
Her romantic hopes died as he screamed and he cried
while calling out loud for his mother.

The manager beckoned her over to say
everyone knows the games tough,
But I think you should know you'll just have to go,
the boys think you're playing too rough.

Now Maggie is feeling rejected, she tries harder
than any girl can
to take as a lover anyone's brother, in fact,
any kind of a man.

Changing her tactics is crucial if she has
any kind of a chance,
She pondered the joys of an armful of boys
So took herself off to a dance.

Satin blouse straining over her biceps,
high heels crunching the floor,
She wants to be seen as Disco-ing Queen,
in the arms of one man, or a score.

She fluttered her eyes at the menfolk as
she twirled one man over her head,
But there, where no male smiles at her womanly wiles,
They just envied her muscles instead.

Then onto the floor stepped Metallic Mick,
a wrestler who'd won every prize,
Her heart beat too fast, she had found him at last
the moment she looked in his eyes.

Round his neck he wore a circle of steel
which shone with a dazzling ray,
And the diesel like fume of his macho perfume
Took all of her senses away.

He held out his hand and she took it, saying
'Lady, let's dance for a while'
Without any qualms she fell into his arms
as he flashed her a metallic smile.

He whirled her around, 'till his feet left the ground,
While hers stayed firm on the floor,
One little flip, had him in a death grip,
then she planted a kiss on his jaw.

He breathlessly told her he'd just have to leave
for a meeting with friends across town,
Re-aligning his jaw, he heads for the door,
But Maggie is wearing a frown.

His fans where holding a party that day,
celebrating their Champion killer,
So he was very keen, not to be seen in
arms of this lady gorilla.

Maggie's arms are now empty, and so is her heart,
another man's left her behind,
But she's not a person to whimper and moan,
She was never the worrying kind.

Inviting herself to his party, deciding she
needed some bliss,
She bursts through the door, tackles him to the floor,
then hoovers him up with a kiss.

From her handbag she pulls out a magnet,
of huge industrial size,
One mighty click magnetized Metal Mick,
see the panic well up in his eyes.

We all know she longed for a lover, trying
harder than any girl can,
So while she holds onto the magnet,
Maggie has hold of her man.

Life's Changes

I listened as he spoke a while,
his voice was frail and sad,
He'd phoned to tell a radio show
of the lonely life he had,
The presenter listened patiently
as he told about his life,
He'd survived his friends, but sadder still
he'd survived his darling wife,

His carer thought computers might
fill his empty days,
Where he would find new online friends,
if he could change his ways,
But what good are online friends to me
if I can't touch a hand,
Or have smiling eyes that look at me
to show they understand.

Or to feel warm arms around me,
know that reassuring touch,
these are the things I hunger for,
and miss so very much.
But thank you dear for listening,
You have been very kind.
I just had to say this modern world
has left me far behind.

Night Shade

Night draws her cloak about us
But it is frayed and thin,
While she tries to mend the holes
The evening sun looks in.

He pokes through long gold fingers
And tries to feel about,
He plays this game until he's tired,
Then all the stars peep out.

Dancing Dilemma

Passing a dancehall I heard the sweet strains
of a beautiful old fashioned tune,
Enticed by the music I wandered towards it
and shyly peered into the room,

I chose not to wait for an invite to dance,
So stepped into this musical stream,
And was lifted up high on wings of sweet sound
as though in a wonderful dream.

Whirling and twirling on fast flying feet
So merged with the soul of the dance,
Weaving around the bright happy partners
I drown in a hypnotic trance.

This cascading sound stirs me round and around
Such delirious feelings I'm feeling,
Nobody told me that dance was such heaven
I'm spinning and twisting and reeling.

Some of the dancers are smiling, some frowning,
but I'm lost in a feeling so clear,
Up high on this spiritual, magical moment,
A feeling of' 'not being here'

Now the music is waning, the dance it is fading
Leaving a feel of romance,
Then a lady confides as I walk to my seat,
I've hijacked a pensioners dance.

Where's Harry?

Whatever has happened to Harry?
He's disappeared like a big kid.
His teeth in their tumbler are grinning at me
Which is much more than he ever did.

I see something glint in the corner,
And notice it's Harry's glass eye,
I've a suspicion that he is suspicious,
It's probably left there to spy.

His false leg is stood by the window,
Unremembered, it could be his age,
So as he's decided to leave it behind
He must have hopped off in a rage.

There's a dark horrid thing in the bathroom,
It stands there just threatening me,
I beat it with a stick, (you've got to be quick)
Then I find it is Harry's toupee.

I'm accused of betraying our marriage,
He says I been flirting with Dan,
But as Dan's not as handsome as Harry,
I'm thinking he's got the wrong man.

Tea: Celebrating D-Day, British Style

When we watch old war movies, what do we see?
Everyone's guzzling tea.

Backbone of the nation a foe cannot sever,
No matter the bullets, the bombs, or the weather,
As a nation they stood resolutely together
With ladles of sweet scalding tea.

Churchill is calling, he's leading the fray,
His rallying cry is 'We fight come what may',
His words true and good, are stirring the blood,
While the Nation is stirring it's tea.

Tea for the General who's mopping his brow,
Thinking of ways to teach jerry how,
He needs inspiration, they're bringing it now
In a mug full of steaming hot tea.

Then there's the Commander, steering his ship,
A cuppa's the thing for a stiff upper lip,
His crew are defiantly doing their bit
Swigging down oceans of tea.

Dear Daphne! poor Cecil is lost once again,
Those horrible Germans have shot down his 'plane,
He'll be very upset with those jerries I bet
If he misses his afternoon tea.

A surgeon is poised to chop off a leg,
The patient is anxious, he's told not to beg,
Sir! Don't be pathetic, we've no anaesthetic,
But we do have a nice cup of tea.

Hospitals call for transfusions galore,
The nation is primed, for they all know the score,
There is no confusion, the nation's transfusion
British blood, laced with strong British Tea.

Wings

A butterfly did flutter by,
A bee buzzed on it's way
A lark soared high into the sky
To serenade the day.

Their cheerful chorus beckons me
Enticing clear and sweet,
But I can't play
For I must stay
Shackled by two earthbound feet.

Tess's Tale

Tess is a long legged golden girl She moves with speed and grace,
A flash of gold. a pair of heels she's running at a pace,
Squirrels scatter far and fast, it's a game of wits and skill,
The squirrel's happy to survive, but Tess is out to kill,

She jumps around on long gold legs as though to climb the tree,
Barking loud as if to say, 'Come down and 'play' with me',
We found this lethal lady in a place for waifs and strays,
A place where sadly we were told that some dogs end their days.

Tess was pleased with her new home, she bounced from chair to chair.
Then lay down in her cosy bed and slept without a care,
We're told she'd been a hunting dog, which had caused her to survive,
The skills she'd learned to hunt and kill had helped her stay alive.

How can we change this hunting dog into a family pet?
teach her new ways to remember, and old ways to forget.
At home she's very gentle, with a passion for her food,
So we fill her up, now she's slowed down,
The squirrels think that's good.

The Journeyman

Please sir, do you have a bed?
I've walked a long, long way
Somewhere I can rest my head
and dream until bright day,

It's taken much to bring me here,
A road of endless miles,
and I have paid the price I fear,
it's paved in sadness, paved with smiles.

I've watched the dawn of humankind
and wondered at it's birth,
some moved ahead, (some left behind)
to spread across the earth.

I've seen the rise of pyramids
and watched man enslave man,
where one man does as one man bids.
To cage him if he can.

A bright soul came to tell of love
unconditional was it's name
'Don't be the tiger be the dove',
He died in graceful pain.

I've watched the world keep turning,
the ages passing by.
what lessons are we learning?
we die still wondering why.

The scenery and the costumes change
but man has stayed the same,
and he will try hard to arrange
that someone takes the blame.

Accept me, a weary stranger,
Give some shelter if you can,
don't fear that I bring danger,
for I am you, and everyman.

A Close Shave

Dwelling inside Alfie Arnett's insides
was the keeper of Alf's dodgy liver,
The state of the organ was causing concern,
it was tired, and had started to wither,

He confides in the keeper of Alfie's lame heart
which was in a bad way, just the same,
So they both called the manager down from Head office,
(Who was trying to jolt Alfie's brain,)

They are feeling defeated by Alf's appetites
as they watch their host's arteries throb,
if they fail to come up with a happy solution
all three will be out of a job.

A solution was found, out of sheer desperation
They voted to come out on strike.
And force the said Alf to give up his lifestyle
to stop eating the food he might like.

So now Alf is picking at food meant for rabbits.
And that's how it's going to stay.
He took a bad turn when his keepers downed tools,
He's fed up.. but alive to this day.

The Gentleman

Walking through a local park, I saw him sitting there
elderly, and quite alone. His clothes a touch threadbare,
His hat, broad brimmed and battered, sat squarely on his head
In his hands he held his lunch, a meagre slice of bread.

I felt to move towards him. Offer money, show I care,
But there was 'something' in his manner, he had a certain air.
There was a dignity about him. It was his only wealth
for shabby was his whole attire, and shabby was his health

So there he sat unnoticed, watching people as they pass,
And even though he's frail and old, he has a touch of class.

Night Time Serenade

Lying in my bed one night
Fast asleep with eyes shut tight,
A sound disturbed my slumbering,
is it a song. Does someone sing?

The hour is late, (I feel a scowl)
a time when only tomcats prowl
but this insomniac dares to keep
late hours and disrupt my sleep,

I leave my bed to stand and glare,
The warbler doesn't have a care
it's obvious he doesn't see
grumpy curtain twitching me.

I watch him staggering alone,
drunkenly weaving his way home,
his booze filled voice does rise and fall,
with bouncing echoes off each wall.

He's singing to the empty street,
on two intoxicated feet,
I listen, 'til the drunken sound
grows fainter as he's homeward bound.

So now I'm back to what is real
the night time holds an empty feel,
My boozy friend has found his home,
and suddenly I feel alone.

Missed Me

The day is fine, I'll cut the grass,
(It's not my favourite chore)
There are so many other things
that manage not to bore.

Will I come across an elephant?
It's been growing for a while,
Or maybe sly Lord Lucan,
but our gardens not his style.

I push the mower to and fro
as well as I am able,
Good grief! will you just look at that
It's like a billiard table.

Satisfied, I go indoors to make a cup of tea,
Then look to see one blade of grass
Staring back at me.

Reflections on a Park Bench

Ted Tatworth wondered were life might be going
as he sat on a bench in the park,
Life seemed to happen, rather than planning,
and today he's as much in the dark.

'The 'missus' seems happy', he said to himself,
and the kids have far more than they need,
The cat and the dog have a full happy life,
There's only me going to seed.'

He looked at the message inscribed on the bench,
'For Donald, who's loved and much missed',
and he wondered what message would sum up his life,
'To Ted, who just longed to be kissed',

'I don't want to be seen as a bench in the park
donated by my darling wife,
As things are there won't be a great deal of change,
I've been sat on for most of my life.'

Happy Home

There's a house in the hills we are eyeing,
It seems more of a home than a house,
it's time we invested, it isn't infested with
beetles, or bugs, or the mouse.

It's standing on solid foundations,
and seems to be wearing a smile,
So perhaps we should try it,I think we might buy it,
And live there a very long while.

The garden is fine from a distance,
Up close it's a mountain of weeds,
The fence is a fright, but we'll soon put it right
with some back breaking gardening deeds.

But it's the house that's attracting attention,
it's warm and it's cosy and bright
So if I say please, will you fetch me the keys,
I'd like to move in by tonight.

Night Visitor

Lying in my bed one night
I woke up startled, stiff with fright,
Then strained to see what could it be
that's fallen down the chimney.

Enveloped in a cloud of soot,
appearing to be downside up,
It coughed and sneezed, let out a wheeze;
'Who are you'? I asked grimly.

A voice said 'I'm so sorry dear
There really is no need to fear,
To put it plain I missed my aim
My eyes see rather dimly'.

Are you the one I came to find?
Sometimes I've too much on my mind
I visit Venus, visit Mars,
spend lots of time amongst the stars.
I spread myself too thinly.

I know you're going to say that's rich,
but I am the appointed witch,
Who grants a wish and casts a spell,
I'm told I do it very well,
Just ask my boyfriend Finlay.

I thought about it for a while,
It might be great to change my style,
I chased the thought around my head.
but when I toppled out of bed.
She vanished up the chimney.

The View

We were a little group all on our own,
The guns were spraying wild around our head,
Laid low,(our fiercest wish to stay alive)
So hid amongst the bodies of the dead.

The captain's voice cut clear above the din,
Men hold your nerve, stay close, and follow me,
We moved as one, we breathed as one, and then
a bullet struck, our little group was three,

We turned to find the captain lying prone,
I watched the life light fading in his eyes,
He asked that I would lead our ragged few,
I nodded, and then I heard his dying sighs.

We turned towards the killers of our man,
If we should die, it will not be in vain,
For King, for captain, we three climbed the rise
To fall back dying, as the bullets rain.

Two Slippers

I'm leaving you Stan, I've found a new man,
one with a pulse and a brain.
He's cheerful and funny with plenty of money,
and doesn't think life is a pain.
So! I'm leaving for sure you mind numbing bore,
I'm tired of this menial life,
Tired of cooking you kippers, and fetching your slippers,
I'm more like your mother than wife.
My mind's turned to jelly watching you watch the telly,
You've developed a Frankenstein stare,
Just take it from me, anybody can see
you've become the same shape as that chair.

I'm glad you said that you sarcastic old cat,
if you'll give me permission to speak,
So I'll make myself clear, it'll please you to hear
I've had my bags packed for a week.
I've found a young lady whose loving and kind,
she works at the Old Hop and Vine,
Her voice doesn't' leave scorch marks on my ears,
Her moustache isn't bigger than mine.

Why you lecherous fart!! Not that sex mad old tart,
The one that folk call Bizzy Lizzy,
Why I hear from our Jack she lives on her back,
So that when she stands up, she gets dizzy.

For a minute there Flo', I saw the pink glow
in your cheeks, Like when you were a lass,
You were dimpled and sweet; you were light on your feet,
You were my girl, with oodles of class,

Well! I stifled a sigh at the fire in your eye,
A fire that used to burn bright,
Shall I cook you some kippers? Yeh! Pass me my slippers
And I'll see what's on telly tonight.

The Riddle

I'm not what you think, I'm myself in disguise,
I've come here to capture the ultimate prize,
Don't believe what you see with your frail human eyes,
What they 'see' as the truth, is the Mother of lies.

The Spook

The castle is tall.. the night is dark,
I catch the gleam of a flickering spark,
and take a step towards the light
that seems to dance in the dead of night.

Many souls must haunt this place
who've often died in deep disgrace,
they leave a sense of stark despair
that wraps around the walls ... the air.

Should I dare to track its path
Would I hear a ghoulish laugh,
Then realisation knocks me flat,
it's a reflector collar on an old tomcat.

The Keeper

The Ghost of Grimly Castle's Keep
was never ever known to sleep,
Jealously he prowls the walls,
the corridors and banquet halls,
So he was in a towering rage,
when persons of the pimple age
dared set foot in his domain,
their very presence gave him pain.

He eyed the pair, a sallow knave
who might have crawled out of a cave,
The other did bemuse his mind,
was it a wench?, a trousered kind?
'Ho there knave, why come you here?
Take heed I'll give thee cause to fear
Take thy wench and hence depart,
or I will freeze thy rascals heart',

What meanest thou 'get stuffed old man'?,
pray speak in English if you can,
What sign is this, two fingers raised?
such strange behaviour leaves me fazed.
Should I perceive this as a slur.?
then thou't shall pay thou weaselly cur,
Pestilence!, be fleet of foot..
begone or I will crack thy nut.

As he raged the Keep did quake,
so much anger did he make,
The 'knave' and 'wench' rose up and ran,
fearful of the 'weird old man',
His anger tore into each wall..
and soon the keep begins to fall,
No more a part of kingly homes..
instead he guards a pile of stones.

Samson (Remodeled)

Samson was a mighty man,
twice as strong as my old gran,'
The secret of his strength so rare,
was in his long and curly hair
All type of barbers shops he'd shun,
and kept his hair tied in a bun.

One thing scared this lusty lad,
t'was not the Philistines or his Dad,
Nor was it Beasts who roamed the night
that made our Samson stiff with fright,
It was Delilah with her shears
which brought the the poor man close to tears,
He'd rather by the beasts be mauled
than have that woman clip him bald.

One night she took him out to dine,
and filled him up with Goosegog wine,
Whilst Sam was sleeping off his greed,
Delilah did a dirty deed,
You've read the books and all that's said
of how Sam came by his bald head,
How up to Samson she did sneak,
chopped off his curls and left him weak,

Gone were his curls he looked a fright,
now't to shampoo each friday night
And where his muscles once did quiver,
began to slip and slide and wither.
The Philisties to Sams surprise,
took turns at poking out his eyes,
That wasn't right, it wasn't fair,
'cos now he had no eyes or hair.

He realised his friends weren't true,
they shouted 'Heavens ! look at you
You can't be seen in broad day light,
you're giving all the girls a fright'.
He hid away for months, or more,
'till his locks returned just as before,
So hurt was Sam left in the lurch,
he went and wrecked the local church,
Delilah, looking very dead,
wished she hadn't shaved his head.

Wondering

Was it you that I saw, sitting all by yourself
with a faraway look in your eye?
Were you happy or sad, were the thoughts good or bad
in the tears as you started to cry?.

Is it someone you love, or maybe have loved
that leaves you in this state of mind,?
But whatever the reason, whoever the person
I hope that the memories are kind.

Sweet Flight

Fly from my heart sweet labour of my love.
Then take that love to shape a love filled life,
For you are grown from happiness, and dreams
My dream for you to soar above cold strife.

But should the stones of life bruise your soft wings
remember life that loves you tells you clear
swoop higher on hearts music, then you'll find
a song that takes you where there is no fear.

The love that lifts you up must bring you home.
Stay bright, stay strong where ever you may roam.

Devotion

He's a mild mannered man, not easy to rouse,
Who liked to live quietly in his little house.
He prided himself on his gardening skill,
though some find it boring, it gave him a thrill,

Seeing his rhubarb grow healthy and strong
was the thing that he worked for all the day long.
But the one thing that pleased him, he called it his prize.
were his marrow-fat peas as big as your eyes.

Coming home from the market with a bag of manure
are there sounds in the garden? He has to make sure,
Then standing stock still, he's too dumb for words,
finds gobbling his prize peas, a flock of big birds,

Our man's seeing red , he's mild mannered no more,
He runs for his shotgun, he's looking for gore.
Taking aim at the varmints, eyeballs bulging red,
He misses the thieves, but his rhubarb is dead.

A Wish

I looked into the eyes of the future,
He had just turned seven years old,
his eyes were wide, an inquisitive green,
His hair shone a burnished gold,

I watched him play in the sunlight,
he leaped and whooped and ran,
his essence was joy this golden boy,
and I caught a glimpse of the man,

Would life let the man be as joyful,
let him keep that inquisitive mind.
will his spirit fly free as a spirit should be,
and his heart stay as happy and kind.

Homeless

Night lay cold about the town,
the moon kept vigil in the sky.
Upon the air no sound was heard
save the moaning of the wind,
It's icy breath arresting life,
incarcerating it in ice,
Imprisoned, like a frosty hell
awaiting mortals who have sinned.

The icy silence broken now
by footfalls near a withered tree,
A figure huddled, tired, and bent,
treading o'er the wintry earth.
With clothes well worn, it's life near spent,
wills itself along the way
Cursing hard it's sorry life,
wondering why t'was given birth.

One foot forward one behind,
blackened, bleeding, blue with cold,
The toes peeped through a broken shoe
no cobbler knew or cared to mend,
Tattered rags that trail the ground
wearily upon the stones
Is all that's needed, t'would suffice
to see their master to his end.

His breath trails out behind him
fluttering like a ghostly hand,
As evidence that life was still
inhabiting the frame,
Clinging in defiance
of all that wished him ill.
Yet wishing life would end its cruel game.

The broken shoes tread dutifully
Winter's hardened shell,
The moon shines cold upon the shriveled form
Who searches with a desperate eye,
a hollow soft and dry,
To shelter him, until he meets
tomorrow's frozen morn.

Survival

Believe me when I tell you that
I own a big electric cat,
My dad, who makes things of this sort.
could see me looking rather fraught,
For one determined beastly mouse
was busy chewing up my house.

It chewed up carpets, doors, and cheese.
I found a hole in my deep freeze,
Just when I think things can't get worse,
he's chewing on my favourite purse.

He ate the shoes of my best friend
now here I am at my wits end
So just to stop me going grey,
dad stepped in and saved the day,

His ingenuity and skill invented Sparks, who's born to kill,
With nails for teeth, and nails for claws,
he's dealing death without a pause,
This mouse creating furry hell.
I call the Scarlet Pimpernel

We seek him here, we seek him there
but he chews on without a care
It's clear the reckoning is nigh..
Now's the time to say goodbye,

I switch on Sparks, his eyes shine bright,
at least he'll give the mouse a fright,
The banging, clanging, squeaking sound,
says Sparks has mousey brought to ground,

So now the mouse has upped and died.
but strange to say the family cried.

The Duel

The devil looked me in the eye,
I looked at him the same,
He tried to bend me to his will.
I would not play his game,

You've had your own way far too long
I'm too long in your spell,
I told the keeper of the dark,
The keeper of my hell,

From this day on my hell's my own
for me to understand,
Not some vague terror you have shown
to tie me to your hand,

I am the master of the fears
That I must come to know
and should I come to love that fear
Your power is dealt a blow.

Lost Friend (Charlie Died)

One misty moistly morning when the world seemed soaked in dew,
I thought I'd take some exercise and walk a mile or two,
As I walked the mist grew dense, and soon became a fog,
Not only did I lose my way, I'd lost our family dog.

Creeping along I called out loud, but heard no answering bark,
We both were lost in what should be the old familiar Park,
I wandered wide, I wandered far, to cover lots of ground,
I searched hard for my furry friend; he's nowhere to be found,

A Pub looms up out of the fog, I step inside to see
My missing pooch lies by the fire looking back at me,
He's gobbling treats, he wags his tail; he's smiling with his eyes,
Our Charlie's made himself at home in doggie paradise.

Ghostly Doings

I am the ghost of twelve oclock
I haunt the mansion stairs,
Sometimes I haunt all on my own,
sometimes we haunt in pairs.

It thrills my bones, when men yell out,
While ladies hide and scream,
And should they fall down in a faint,
that really makes me keen.

One time, the ghost of Wormwood Hall
was sickly for a spell,
So on the odd occasion
I haunt that place as well.

The Duke of Bedlam has no head,
The Headsman chopped it off,
But as he suffers with his chest
It's hard for him to cough.

Then Lady Hardup..so I hear,
will only haunt the rich,
she did so in her lifetime
She never owned a stitch.

So when the hour turns midnight,
and I've had my tea and toast.
You must beware if on the stair,
You see the midnight ghost.

Soul Dance

I am filled with the joy of the dance I am dancing
with you and the music, the night is a dream,
We are floating on sounds that are lighter than whispers,
Caught up in an endlessly magical scene.

We stepped into the music the night of our meeting,
we knew we had danced to this music before
in many lives past, and now into the future,
though our future bring sorrows our joy is the more.

Wanderlust

I watched a film the other night,
The heroine was shy but bright,
The hero loved his lady fair with
bright blue eyes, and flaxen hair,

But he was restless, and she found
he didn't like to hang around,
He told his darling 'come with me'
and so they both took off to sea,

Our hero was the proudest dad,
because they had a little lad,
Who went along just for the fun,
to where there's lots of sand and sun,

In Africa they made the grade,
and that's the reason why they stayed,
They both worked hard, and found some friends,
But that's not where the story ends,

Our hero kissed his darling wife,
Then crashed his car and lost his life,
The lady suffers more heartache
Her son is bit by his pet snake.

She's left to mourn bereft and sad,
and laid her boy beside his dad.
But she's a girl as tough as boots,
and carries on her mans pursuits.

It's comforting to see her thrive
the only one that's left alive,
I'm pleased my man don't like to roam,
We'll die of boredom safe at home.

War: 1914 – 1918

They've stared into the fires of hell,
and looked the 'devil' in the eye
who bids the war lords come to blows,
all watch and grieve as young men die,
Seeing how he breathes out hate
See how tyrants breathe it in
disguised as saviours, tell the masses,
'Follow me, and we can win'.

They tread a carpet of the dead,
to wade through seas of precious blood,
plundered from the young and brave
at a time when life was good,
The 'devils' eyes like moulten fire,
scorch the earth for miles around,
Echoed in the thundering guns
that spit out flame to split the ground.

As the source of all that's hate
takes it's fill of human fear,
So they surrender trembling souls,
to sacrifice all that's held dear,
While the 'Lord of Darkness' rules..
our lives will be the darkest night
because of fear, our eyes are blind,
and cannot see our home, the light.

Listening

An Angel fell out of the sky yesterday,
She'd bruised her wing on a black cloud
She was coming to rescue someone in pain
They were calling for help rather loud.

I rushed over to give her angelic first aid
soothing oils from my best crystal dish,
and a plaster to stick her bruised feathers together.
She smiled, and said; 'What do you wish.?'

I thought for a moment, my mind was a blank
'I can't think of a wish for myself,
so I wished for world peace, but she shook her bright head.
"Til men listen, that wish stays on the shelf."

Reunion: The Eternal Fight Between Light and Darkness

I saw the face of darkness
engaged in every fight,
at its core was longing
For reunion with the light.

The giving hand of light reached out,
but ignorance held back,
Should it try to take that hand
It, too, might be stained black,

You are the key to all my fears
the answers I must know,
If you that's light become the dark,
Then where am I to go?

I am the life in everything
I live in every cell,
Within the dark, within the light,
I live in you as well,

You are but a shadow self
that dwells in fear and strife,
You hold the keys to mortal death,
I hold the keys to life,

I'm brighter than ten million suns
And you are but a spark,
It's easy to switch on a light,
you can't switch on the dark,

If we should blend, the spark in you
will flood the light that's me,
Then the answers to our questions
will set your knowledge free.

A Walk in the Woods

Strolling through the wood one night,
I thought I saw an eerie light
and something sounding like a drum,
that had a kind of witchy hum

Hair on end, I tiptoe near,
trying not to feel the fear,
Then saw two figures dancing wild
just like Mother Natures child.

Both of them were in the buff,
dancing hard and dancing rough,
Flesh was flashing all around
To the hypnotic drumming sound.

I could only stand and stare
at boobs and backsides everywhere,
What mystery did this invite?
I can't say it's a pretty sight.

Then as I sought to turn away
feeling it's better not to stay,
The mysteries solved, that's when I saw
Aunt Aggie, and the man next door.

A Double Life

Mrs. Millicent Madeleine Murgatroyd Smith
Was terribly tired in the day,
If her friends should invite her out for a meal
They found she had nothing to say.

For instead of engaging with this friend or that
She'd yawn and her eyelids would droop,
So the friends were alarmed to find Mrs Smith
Falling face first in the soup.

Her friends became anxious, 'What's happened to her
Is she lacking in iron and such,?
She must need a tonic to bolster her up,
She's falling about far too much!

They take her to bed for an afternoon nap,
She wakens at six on the dot,
As a pensioner she must find things to do
So has taken a pole dancing spot.

Donning her corsets, she tightens the strings
With the aid of a nearby door knob,
She tugs and she pulls 'till she feels the right size
And her eyeballs have started to throb.

Feeling fifty years younger she heads for the door
To give all her public a treat,
She pictures them screaming, and shouting bravo!
Whilst throwing pound notes at her feet.

The lessons she learned at the pole dancing class
Are applied with passion and zeal,
The steam she gives off while working her moves
Even an old corpse could feel.

With a hand knitted veil to add some mystique
She attempts to dazzle and tease,
But the loud clapping noise which she takes for applause
is the sound of her arthritic knees

She twangs her suspender at an old man nearby
He immediately grabs his inhaler,
Her erotic contortions all over the place
Causes his face to grow paler.

The medics were called and carried him out.
(he'd seen far too much in the war)
But the sight of that gyrating mountain of flesh
Had left his nerve endings quite raw.

Flashing her varicose veins at the crowd,
She teases, she taunts, and she flirts,
Wriggling and twisting herself 'round the pole,
Dancing all night 'til it hurts.

The crowd, mesmerised by the gobsmacking sight.
Stare as their eyeballs grow sore,
Until the said pole gave up the ghost,
And fell with a crash to the floor.

Now the shows over, she gave them her all,
Fulfilled she goes home to her bed,
She collides with the milkman who hands her a pint,
Soon she's snoring, and sleeps like the dead.

Mrs Millicent Madeleine Muratroyed Smith
Was terribly tired in the day...................

Twilight

A setting sun..looks like the world's on fire
with crimson rays that flood the evening sky,
Birds! blackened silhouettes against this fiery glow
seek out their nests, to where they can retire.

This is the magic hours that we call twilight,
when day winds down with one last glorious fling
to slow its breath, the evening brings a feeling
of quietening now, and birds have ceased to sing.

Nights blanket folds around the bright of daylight
extinguishing it's warm and rosy ray,
And now the raucous hours leave off their clamour
To bring a calm surrender of the day.

The Child

When the child inside is crying like a baby,
because of 'things' that happened when we were very small,
Now we've become a grownup and simply cannot own up
to why we cannot feel grownup at all.

When debris from the past has left us lonely
because untutored 'adults' have filled us with their fears,
so the ignorance of their past, which they cling to 'til the last
is our inheritance, fulfilled in empty years.

There's an answer.. if we recognise the meaning
Become the 'adult' who can turn our life around,
Although it may sound wild.. we must become our favourite child,
and soon we'll find our life's on solid ground.

Life's Song

While glancing across the room,
their eyes met.. a glance that caused
them to meet on every level of their being,

Here in the flesh, was the missing part of the other,
Words had found the music..
From that second.. life became the sweetest song.

No Shelter Here

As wintry weather worms its way
into the old mans bones,
Its icy fingers make his flesh
and limbs feel cold as stones,
The thin and shabby clothes
he wears do naught to stay the cold,
which punishes the homeless,
but much more when you are old.

Thoroughbred

Look at that horse! I'm watching him go
He's just getting into his stride,
He's building up speed and I've no doubt at all
there's a touch of class he cannot hide.

This magnificent 'Shire' is 'going for gold'
not hindered by weight or by size,
He's up and away, he's seizing the day
with a determined look in his eyes.

He's jumping the ditches, He's leaping the hedges
He's running as though he's on fire!
Tearing through forests he scatters the wildlife
There's no sign that he'll ever tire,

The style of the horse! the heart of the horse!
He must be the thoroughbred kind,
It's amazing to see that he isn't slowed down
by the milk cart he's pulling behind.

I Can Fly

Out for a walk amongst like-minded people,
I spotted a church with a very high steeple,
Suddenly! longing to be in its tower
I climbed up the stairs, (it took me an hour)

I arrive at the top, the view was immense,
This beautiful space invades every sense,
A feast for the senses, food for the eye,
A feeling of love, so much I can fly,

I leap through the air, then I'm prompted to think
Maybe I shouldn't have had that last drink.

Author's Biography

I am divorced, and the proud mother of a son and daughter, who are now both grown and successful, I worked for a charity 'The Samaritans' helping people with their varied problems, (in interview or over the phone,) which gave me an insight into people and myself, This encouraged me into writing this book, telling of the fun, the individuality and Spirituality of us all Later moving back to England, and Derbyshire, we made new freinds, I rediscovered poetry, which is a 'legacy' from my Grandmother, who. when I was small would give me Nursery Rhyme Books, for Christmas or Birthdays, which stayed with me to this day, I hope you enjoy the people in the pages, You might find yourself there??

Please Review!

All independent authors depend upon reviews left on
Amazon.com by readers to help promote their books.
Without these reviews, they will hardly get any notice.
Please take the time to leave a short review.
Simply go to Amazon.com, find the book and go to the
book's page. Under the author's name will be a list of reviews
and stars. Click here and there will be a big button saying
"Create your own review". Please click here and review.

It only takes a minute!

*Keep up with the latest poetry
by Maureen Higson on Allpoetry.com*

A Village Poetry People Available at the Allpoetry Bookstore!